GW00777595

Nihil obstat

John M. A. Fearns, S.T.D.

Censor Librorum

Imprimatur

✠ Francis Cardinal Spellman,

Archbishop of New York

December 4, 1946.

Letters of St. Gemma Galgani

Edited by
Fr. Germano of St. Stanislaus,
Passionist.

Translated from the Italian by
The Dominican Nuns of
Corpus Christi Monastery,
New York City.

Our Lady's Home

New York City
1947

COPYRIGHT DEPOSIT.

FOREWORD

To those unacquainted with the life story of St. Gemma Galgani, some little introduction may be welcome.

She was born on March 12, 1878, at Camigliano, a small town in the neighborhood of Lucca, Italy. From her earliest years she was an angel of piety and innocence. When Gemma became of school age the family moved to Lucca and her education was confided to the Sisters of St. Zita. Her mother died when she was but eight years old.

In 1897 her father's death occurred, and the following year Gemma herself fell dangerously ill. This period of her life marks the beginning of the extrordinary mystical graces which characterize her spiritual life. She was miraculously cured through the intercession of St. Gabriel, and was favored by several apparitions of this saint.

Not only St. Gabriel, but her Guardian Angel, the Blessed Virgin, and Our Lord appeared to her and spoke to her. The Evil One himself was also among her visitors and he left nothing undone to torment and terrify her.

She bore on her body the marks of the stigmata, and also those of the crown of thorns. Every week, between Thursday night and Friday afternoon, she went through all the sufferings of the Sacred Passion.

Because of the uncongenial atmosphere of her own home, and in obedience to the wishes of Our Lord, Gemma accepted, in 1899, the invitation of the Giannini family to come and make her home with them. Here she was loved and respected even to the point of veneration. Her place in the family was that of an adopted daughter.

When, in 1902, Gemma developed tuberculosis, the Giannini family were advised by the doctor to send her away in order to safeguard the health of their own children. They delayed long in doing so, but finally, in January, 1903, they rented a room for her in a neighboring house and prevailed upon one of her aunts to act as her nurse. Here Gemma died, in the arms of a member of the Giannini family on April 12, 1903, which, that year, was Holy Saturday.

The following letters are only a few of the one hundred and fifty or so collected by Padre Germano. As Gemma never dated a letter, it is not possible to give them in chronological order.

Gemma's confessor during practically the whole of her life was Msgr. Volpi, who later became Bishop of Arezzo. In order that he might not be alone in the guidance of this highly favored soul, he asked and obtained the assistance of Padre Germano, a Passionist priest whose ordinary place of residence was Rome. Business of one kind or another relating to his Congregation often brought him to Lucca. While there he was a guest of the Giannini family and it was here that he was an eye-witness of Gemma's extraordinary holiness.

Though the visits of Padre Germano to Lucca were frequent, Gemma's ordinary intercourse with him was by means of letters, every one of which he preserved, though not all have been given to the public. They deal with all the various phases of her spiritual life and reveal the saint to us just as she was,—simple as a child, lovable, human, and deeply sympathetic with every form of human woe.

PART ONE

TO HER DIRECTOR

(PADRE GERMANO)

CONTENTS

I. She begins timidly to open her heart to her new director, who is a stranger. 1

II. Salutary reflections and precious fruit drawn from constant meditation on eternal truths. 3

III. Disgust with the world; joy at being despised and humiliated; longing for still greater perfection. 5

IV. She humbles herself for having felt some repugnance in obeying. 6

V. She fears being in a state of illusion. 7

VI. She grieves over having been subjected to a physical examination. 8

VII. Having learned that her director was at the tomb of St. Gabriel, she asks for prayers. 10

VIII.   On another occasion she once more
        urges an embassy to St. Gabriel.   11

IX,   She enjoys such liberty of spirit in
        regard to earthly things that she
        cannot find any attachments.   13

✠   ✠   ✠

LETTERS OF
ST. GEMMA

I. SHE BEGINS TIMIDLY TO OPEN HER HEART
TO HER NEW DIRECTOR, WHO IS
A STRANGER.

Padre:- All that I write is written simply through obedience, and with the greatest repugnance. In regard to all those things which it seems to me that I see and hear every day, I feel the greatest pain; but the command has been given and that comes before everything.

Last night, when I went to pray before Jesus in the Blessed Sacrament, I heard someone call me,- it seemed to me that it was Jesus. (Padre, before you read any further, I beg you, for charity's sake, not to believe anything, anything at all: I write only to obey; otherwise, I would not have said a single word about what follows.) He said to me:- "Daughter, write to that Father whom your confessor wishes. Do it because it is My desire."

"But Jesus" I replied, "do I understand Thee? Do You wish the Father to know everything that concerns me?"

I was about to continue, but it seemed to me that Jesus (or rather, my own head) would not let me, for He

1

said: "That is My will from now on."

When I heard this I was no longer able to speak and Jesus, so it seemed to me, continued:-

"Daughter, blind obedience, perfect obedience, that is the first thing to remember." He added:- "You must be as a dead body; everything that they would have you do, do it promptly. In these days you shall do nothing without first asking counsel of Me."

Padre, for charity's sake, don't believe a word of all this. In order to write you these things I have to do such violence to myself, but I have wished to obey.

This morning, after Holy Communion, Jesus seemed to let me feel His presence. Padre, what moments! But, after a short time, all was over. I kept repeating to Jesus "My Jesus!" I was not able to express myself very well, but Jesus understood.

Bless me and pray very much for

Poor Gemma.

II. SALUTARY REFLECTIONS AND PRECIOUS
FRUIT DRAWN FROM CONSTANT
MEDITATION ON ETERNAL VERITIES.

And now, Padre, listen to my heart! Although Jesus
has made me cry, still He always wishes my good and He
makes me realize it only too well. Listen to what I am
obliged to do when I am with others and they speak of
Jesus, or heaven, or any such thing. Sometimes I am o-
bliged to run away and hide: often I have to beg the one
who is speaking to change the conversation, otherwise I
feel as though I should die. But no. I shall not die yet,
Jesus seemed to say to me:-"No, you will not die now."
I will not stop now to tell you more, you already know
all about this.

Padre, do you know the latest idea that has come into my head? It is to become a saint at all costs. I made
this resolution yesterday evening. During my meditation
I was thinking:- one lives only once; it is certain that one
shall die; and then one has to answer to God. And I know
that this God punishes the wicked with eternal fire.

This malediction, Padre, causes me such fear. For
the love of Jesus, send me your Angel to drive away the

demon (whom, with the help of our Blessed Mother, I have overcome during the past two days;) and beg Jesus to give me the grace to fight victoriously. After my many sins I have learned that Jesus is a real father, full of mercy. How is that? If I, after so many sins, do not know that the goodness of the Heart of Jesus is more than paternal, I must have lost my reason! And what a heart is mine! At last the light has dawned upon my soul; I see how much harm I have done by sin.

Ah! When I see Jesus in tears, it pierces my heart. I realize that I, by my sins, have increased the burden which overwhelmed Him while He prayed in the garden. At that moment Jesus saw all my sins, all my failings, and He saw, also, the place that I should have occupied in hell, if Thy Heart, O Jesus, had not pardoned me

(The following paragraph was written by Gemma in ecstasy, a thing which often happened when she was writing, speaking, or merely listening to someone else speaking of the things of heaven,- as she herself says at the beginning of this present letter. How the family watched over her at these times is explained in her biography.)

Jesus, Jesus, Jesus! No, I will no longer be so sparing of myself, because I wish, with the help of Thy grace, to keep all within me subject to my will. In conclusion, O Jesus, this is my resolution:- I will make reparation to Thee, O Jesus, by treating myself as Thy slave and placing my shoulders beneath Thy cross . . . . O Jesus, my God! . . . I know that he who tries to climb very high slips easily, and falls again into the mud.

Padre, I abandon myself. Bless me at every moment.

Poor Gemma.

III.   DISGUST WITH THE WORLD: JOY AT BEING DESPISED AND HUMILIATED: LONGING FOR STILL GREATER PERFECTION.

Padre. Padre. -- It is always the same Gemma who writes to you. I am still out in the world! But how disgusted I am with it! It is quite right that one should not find happiness upon this earth. If I, through the mercy of God, experience some happy moments, they are when I see myself despised and humiliated.

And of these things, to tell you the truth, there is no

lack. Jesus increases them for me every day. Oh, how good He is! If only you knew what means He has used used in order to humble my pride! Oh, if you but knew how bad I am! Who will ever give me the virtue that I need in order that I may please Jesus? I pray and entreat Jesus to give me in a short time all the helps that I need in order to repair my many miseries, to enlighten my mind, and to let me know the horrible, disgusting state of my soul. And I desire to combine into one all the fervor and love of all holy souls,- or no, better still,- to equal in purity all the angels, and that I may see at last our Mother, Mary most holy.

Bless poor Gemma of Jesus.

IV. SHE HUMBLES HERSELF FOR HAVING FELT SOME REPUGNANCE IN OBEYING.

Padre mio:- May Jesus reward you a thousand times for the great good which your words did to my soul this morning. I am quite resolved to do ever and always the will of my confessor without thinking of what may come of it. If you only knew the great good which your reproof has done me! It is true, every bit of it, what you said to me, and yet there are thoughts which trouble me . . .

It is high time that I should resolve to do the will of my confessor in the future. Every time that I have undertaken something out of my own head, I have paid dearly for it, but now, no, it must no longer be so. I promise not to complain again and not to cry. I will go where my confessor wishes. But it is now already several days since the sacrifice was made.

Once again I wish to thank you for the reproof that you gave me. Do not have any doubt about it; I will know how to profit by it and I want you yourself to see it. Bless me and pray to Jesus for

Poor Gemma.

V. SHE FEARS BEING IN A STATE OF ILLUSION.

Padre:- I am so afraid for my soul! Padre, I am so frightened lest I be in danger of damnation because yesterday I heard a priest, who had come to see Mamma, tell of a nun who had the stigmata on her hands and feet,

head and heart, and who went into ecstacy, too, and it
was all an illusion. And am I like that, Padre? If I deceive others, I shall go to hell. I wish that you would
explain to me just what deceit really is because I do not
wish to deceive anyone. Recommend me to Jesus. I want
to be good and sincere and obedient.

Only the other night there came to me a thought, and
Jesus said to me in the depths of my heart:- "Perhaps
you think that I am incapable of working a miracle either
in regard to yourself or in regard to your confessor?" I do
not understand what is meant, Padre. Ask Jesus to explain it to you.

Bless me. I'll be good.

Poor Gemma of Jesus.

VI. SHE GRIEVES OVER HAVING BEEN SUBJECTED TO A PHYSICAL EXAMINATION.

O Padre, how much I had to suffer yesterday! And
how much these things displeased Jesus! . . . Jesus does
not like this. It was a very great humiliation for me, but
I do not mind.

Jesus is in my heart. This morning I could not go to church and Jesus Himself came to me. He asked me whether He were more lovable in consolation or in humiliation. Padre, how much more lovable He is in humiliation! Here I had Him and there I had my Angel, who, from time to time, presented me a large cross to kiss. How much more lovable He is in humiliation! None of these things trouble me for my own sake, but because of Jesus, because He is not pleased with what took place yesterday evening. On the contrary, He is very much displeased.

And now, Padre, you should see how happy I am with Jesus only, how much more He loves me thus humiliated. Aunt is also very much distressed. I obeyed as best I could and have no ill-will toward anyone, not even the probe. I remained silent. I am happy with only Jesus.

Poor Gemma.

(Gemma sometimes makes use of the word "aunt" and sometimes of "mamma" to designate the pious lady who had adopted her as a daughter.)

VII.   HAVING LEARNED THAT HER DIRECTOR WAS AT THE TOMB OF ST. GABRIEL, SHE ASKS FOR PRAYERS.

Padre mio:- You are doing all that you can in order that you may know what is the true will of God. Then, listen to this, Padre. On the part of Brother Gabriel you have made so many promises. Please do this. Go to his tomb, where his body is, and command him, in the name of obedience:- "Tell me what I must do with regard to Gemma." And then, when you come back, you will write to me, won't you? I will pray as much as I can. Write soon. I will pray very fervently so that Jesus may give you light in my regard, so that you may not be deceived, for charity's sake. . . my God! I am

Poor Gemma.

(In the biography of Gemma a full account is given of her tender and affectionate devotion to St. Gabriel. It was a devotion fruitful in many good works. At the time that these letters were written Padre Germano was working for the beatification of St. Gabriel.

VIII. ON ANOTHER OCCASION SHE ONCE
MORE URGES AN EMBASSY TO
ST. GABRIEL.

By this time I am sure that you have once again had
the good fortune to pray at the feet of Venerable Gabriel.
How I envy you! I have a great many things to tell you,
to be referred to the Saint. First of all, Padre, place in
his hands the important affair of my soul. Ask him if I
may hope to save it. Ask him not to permit me to be deceived, and also not to permit my director to be deceived
in guiding me as he does at present. Kneel and repeat to
him that I have all the good will in the world to save
this poor soul of mine, at the cost of any suffering, any
sacrifice, or humiliation whatsoever. Tell him that, if I
have neglected my soul, please to intercede for me with
Jesus. I ought to have acted differently, I ought to have
taken greater care of my soul because of Jesus and our
Blessed Mother. The hour of repentance ought to have
struck long ago for me, were it not that I am so obstinate
in my sins. Tell him with all your heart to pray to Jesus
not to spare me in the matter of trials. Suffering will up-
lift me spiritually. By abasing me, it will give me the

strength necessary to correspond to the grace of Jesus. Tell him that I am resolved to repair all my past sins, to be obedient, and so on.

O Padre, Padre, beseech him, pray to him like this: ask him to answer these questions:- "Gemma! What ever will become of her? All these things which she seems to see and to hear, whence come they? . . ." I stop here because you know well what I would like to add. For the sake of charity, it won't do any harm if you lose a little time,- if you have other business. Please stay awhile beside Brother Gabriel. Speak to him of me,- of all my affairs. Tell him to send Jesus to me continually, that I am longing to be at the feet of Jesus. Tell him to help me to pray better, beg him to make obedience sweet to me, to obtain for me a little patience. Take a little love from Brother Gabriel and send it to me. There are, then, two things which I recommend especially to you,- first, my soul, and then, all that the future may have in store for me. Padre, I have recommended so many things to you, but you will answer me, won't you? I pray that you may be granted much enlightenment in my regard. Bless me,

Poor **Gemma** of Jesus only.

IX. SHE ENJOYS SUCH LIBERTY IN REGARD TO EARTHLY THINGS SHE CANNOT FIND ANY ATTACHMENTS.

Padre mio:- Listen to this. Every time that I am expecting one of your letters I ask Jesus about it and He tells me:- "It is coming." This last time, as soon as your letter arrived, I went to tell Jesus. "And doesn't he tell you anything?" He asked. "Oh, yes," I replied, "he is constantly recommending me to be humble and detached; but then, the blessed Padre!—he never explains what he means. About being humble, that the confessor explains, but as for being detached, I really do not understand because I no longer have anything. I do not know what there is from which I can detach myself. I have only Thee, my Jesus."

But Jesus,— Padre, do you know what He said?— "That tooth of Ven. Gabriel, tell Me, My daughter, are you not too much attached to that?"

I was silent for a moment and then began to com-

(This tooth was a relic of the Saint and had been given to her by Padre Germano himself.)

plain. "But Jesus," I said, almost in tears, "that is a precious relic!"

And Jesus answered rather seriously, "Daughter, it is thy Jesus Who tells thee so, and that should be sufficient for thee."

Alas, it is true, Padre. Jesus is right. Sr. Maria asked me for it in order to show it to the nuns, and when I had given it to her I cried because I wanted to have it always near me. But Jesus, Jesus, it is to Him that I must be attached ah! Padre mio! Pray always for

Poor Gemma.

The translation of these letters was
made between July 1939, & July 1940.

The type-setting was begun June 2, 1946,
and finished Nov. 25, 1946.

The type used is 8 point Roman
on the Kelsey "Excelsior" press.

This edition consists of sixteen copies,
the present copy being
No. 4

CPSIA information can be obtained
at www.ICGtesting.com
Printed in the USA
BVHW040008160223
658552BV00005BA/138